forsuchatimeasthis

STUDY GUIDE

lisa ryan

Multnomah Publishers

FOR SUCH A TIME AS THIS STUDY GUIDE
published by Multnomah Publishers
A division of Random House, Inc.
© 2003 by Lisa Ryan

International Standard Book Number: 1-59052-174-9

Cover image by Digital Vision
Background cover image by Artville

Unless otherwise indicated, Scripture quotations are from:
The Holy Bible, New International Version © 1973, 1984 by International Bible
Society, used by permission of Zondervan Publishing House

Other Scripture quotations:
New American Standard Bible® (NASB) © 1960, 1977, 1995
by the Lockman Foundation. Used by permission.
The Holy Bible, New King James Version (NKJV)
© 1984 by Thomas Nelson, Inc.
Holy Bible, New Living Translation (NLT) © 1996. Used by permission of Tyndale
House Publishers, Inc. All rights reserved.
The Message © 1993 by Eugene H. Peterson

Multnomah is a trademark of Multnomah Publishers
and is registered in the U.S. Patent and Trademark Office.
The colophon is a trademark of Multnomah Publishers.

Printed in the United States of America

For information:
MULTNOMAH PUBLISHERS
12265 ORACLE BOULEVARD, SUITE 200
COLORADO SPRINGS, CO 80921

06 07 08 09 10—10 9 8 7 6 5

...forsuchatimeasthisstudyguide

I would like to dedicate this to all of the young women—not only here in the United States, but also in China, Ukraine, Latin America, and other parts around the world—who have e-mailed me to express how this message has changed their lives and challenged them to be modern-day Esthers. Many of them have asked me for a companion study guide because they want "more" themselves, or they want to share this with their friends, or they want to start a Bible study group for other young women. *Here is the tool they have asked for.*

TABLE OF CONTENTS

Acknowledgments

I would like to say a big thank-you to Joanne Heim and Renee DeLoriea for helping me make this happen. Also to two of my dearest friends, Kim Newton and Paula Sterns, who encouraged me to continue on and made valuable contributions. With my hectic schedule, my passion for a study guide companion to help young women would not have become a reality without these women.

Getting Started—
How to Use This Guide

Here are a few ideas to help you get the most out of this study.

First, get some friends together. It's more fun to do a study like this one with a group. The Bible is God's Word, and He uses it to tell us stuff like how we should live and act as people who follow Him. That's why it's so important to read and study what we find there—like Esther's story. But God also uses other people to communicate with us. Ever had a friend tell you something that you're pretty sure came straight from God? Going through this study with friends will give God even more opportunity to teach you the things He wants you to learn. People notice different things, and by talking together about what you learn, you'll get much more out of Esther's example.

Second, buy the book *For Such a Time as This* by Lisa Ryan. It will set the stage for the practical lessons in this study. You'll also want to buy a plain journal, index cards, and a box for filing away the index cards.

Third, have a dictionary on hand for looking up definitions of some of the words that will come up in the study.

Fourth, grab your Bible. Some of the verses we'll be looking at closely are printed right here in this book, but you'll want to have a Bible on hand to read all of Esther's story. Plus, as you talk about what you're learning, you may need to hunt around in the Bible to find verses that come to mind or that are brought up in conversation.

Fifth, as you go through the study, you may want to be thinking about putting on an "Esther Banquet." This is a wonderful way to celebrate and share with others your growth as a modern-day Esther. For a few ideas, take a look at the "Hospitality 101" section of week 12.

THE NITTY-GRITTY DETAILS

It's a good idea to find a facilitator—someone to take the lead. Maybe that's you. The facilitator leads the discussion, makes sure everyone knows which sections to do each week, and generally gets things going.

Set a time and place to get together. And don't forget to talk about snacks!

Talk about how long you want to meet. There are thirteen sections in this book, but you could work through two sections at once to do the study in less time. Do what works best for everyone in the group. Finally, when you meet for the first time, it's a good idea to set some ground rules as a group—talk about things like participation (what it means to be part of the group), attendance (how important is it for everyone to be there each time you meet), confidentiality (make sure that what's said in the group stays in the group), and accessibility (how open is everyone to being available to the other members of the group).

That's about it. Let's get started!

It's a Girl Thing

This girl, who was also known as Esther...

ESTHER 2:7

READ CHAPTER 1 IN "FOR SUCH A TIME AS THIS." READ THE BOOK OF ESTHER IN YOUR BIBLE (IT'S SHORT).

There's more to this Old Testament teenager named Esther than just a pretty face. That hardly seems like enough reason to get a whole book in the Bible all to herself. The truth is that Esther *was* more than a pretty face. In fact, after learning more about her, that may end up seeming like the least impressive part of her. Esther's character is what makes her really stand out and shine.

But before we get to her character, the first thing we learn is that she's a girl.

There's tons of stuff out there in the media that tells us what it means to be a woman, a girl—female. Where do you get the most advice about being female?

What are some of the messages you're faced with every day in this culture about how to act, how to look, or how to be because you're a girl?

With all of the messages out there, how do you decide which ones to listen to and which ones to ignore?

WE'RE DIFFERENT

Here's the deal—men and women are different. Seems pretty basic, huh? But the difference between the sexes is greater than just how we look on the outside. God made us different on the inside too, like our emotions, how we think, and what's important to us.

What are some of the "inside" differences between men and women that you notice the most? It might be helpful to make a couple of lists—one about guys, the other about girls.

Think about God's character for a minute—the traits that make Him who He is. How do we as women reflect His character differently than men? Are there certain aspects of God's character that seem particularly "feminine"? Particularly "masculine"?

You have a great opportunity to reflect Christ in ways that guys just can't. Is there one of those characteristics that stands out as something you'd like to work on, a trait you'd like to shine for your non-Christian friends to see?

GIRL POWER!

Throughout history, women have accomplished great things. While not all great women have followed Christ, many have—and found that their greatest power comes from knowing their identity in Christ. As was pointed out in *For Such a Time as This,* "you are a princess in God's court." Wow!

Being a princess—a daughter of the King of kings and Lord of lords— means you're called to a higher standard. What might that mean in your everyday life? Are there specific behaviors or attitudes you need to change so they're suitable for a princess?

How can the friends in this group help you achieve that standard?

Rise Up

You're a woman/girl because God made you one. How can you influence others for God this week by using the distinctly female characteristics He gave you?

For you created my inmost being; you knit me together in my mother's womb. I praise you because I am fearfully and wonderfully made; your works are wonderful, I know that full well. My frame was not hidden from you when I was made in the secret place. When I was woven together in the depths of the earth, your eyes saw my unformed body. All the days ordained for me were written in your book before one of them came to be. (Psalm 139:13–16)

Since writing out Scriptures helps us write them on our hearts, jot down in a journal or on index cards this passage and those that follow in this study. To help you memorize the verses, post them in places where you'll see them often—like on your mirror, in your locker, on the dashboard of your car, and whatnot.

Make it a girl thing by decorating your journal or creating a treasure box for storing your cards. Break out the glue gun, shells, buttons, old jewelry, decoupage—you decide. Like it says in Genesis 2:22, "The Lord God fashioned…woman" (NASB). Fashion your world—it's in your DNA.☺

Radically Pure

Then the king's personal attendants proposed,
"Let a search be made for beautiful young virgins for the king."

ESTHER 2:2

READ CHAPTER 2 IN "FOR SUCH A TIME AS THIS."
READ ESTHER 2:1–4.

When King Xerxes got mad at Queen Vashti, his attendants stepped in and convinced him it was time for a new queen. Here comes the beauty pageant idea—who else but guys would have thought this up? The rules...only beautiful virgins could enter. "The king liked this advice and took it" (Esther 2:4, *The Message*).

Esther's virginity qualified her to move closer to her destiny. The key idea here isn't so much about sex, but about *purity*. Virginity is actually an outward sign of inward purity. And that's what we want to learn from Esther—purity comes from within and transforms everything about who we are.

Grab a dictionary. Look up the following words and write their definitions.

Pure, Purity:

Chaste, Chastity:

Virtuous, Virtue:

Modest, Modesty:

JEZEBEL AND DELILAH

We don't have to look very far to see sex in our society. While it seems over-whelming at times, sex and its distortions are hardly new. Take a few min-utes to read the story of Jezebel in 1 Kings 21:1–16 and 2 Kings 9:30–37. Then read about Delilah in Judges 16:1–21.

How did Jezebel and Delilah use sex and their "girl power" for evil?

How do you see women doing the same thing today?

It can be tempting to use your sensuality to get your way—wearing provocative clothing, flirting, offering or withholding physical affection, and even turning on the tears or a helpless demeanor. Have you ever been tempted to use your power to get your way in something? Have you ever had a conflict of character in a specific situation? When? (You might have to ask the Lord to reveal things you are unaware of.)

What are some specific ways you can reject Delilah's and Jezebel's examples and go for purity instead?

CHOOSE PURITY

Purity is a choice. We have all struggled with purity in some way—whether in our thoughts, our words, or our actions. So how do we get rid of impurity and make a stand for purity?

- Decide to be pure.
- Avoid temptation.
- Set mental boundaries.
- Set physical boundaries.
- Focus on God's Word.
- Spend time with like-minded friends.

If you want to make a choice for purity, it helps to tell others. Who might be some people you could tell about a choice you've made for a life of purity?

It helps to identify our temptations before we face them—that way we can see them coming and avoid them.

Look up 2 Corinthians 7:1. What are some things that lure you away from purity—arousing fiction books, fashion magazines, television programs, movies, being alone with your boyfriend, peer pressure? (Perhaps like one sixteen-year-old who e-mailed me, you are tempted by Internet pornography.)

If you're dating, have you set physical boundaries? If so, have you shared them with the person you're dating?

Friends have the power to keep us on the right track—or to pull us onto the wrong one. What are some ways you can help each other make a stand for purity? Think about things like praying for each other, being honest with your struggles, and encouraging each other. Pick something you can start doing today.

Just as Esther was called to be a Jew in the Persian culture around her, we are called to be Christians in the sex-crazed culture we live in. Consecrating your closet is one way to let your inward call to purity shine through to the outside of your life: Go into your room, turn on some worship music, and ask God to show you any clothing you have that does not project virtue and modesty. Then ask Him to show you other items in your private space—like magazines, CDs, videos, website addresses, and posters—that do not promote a virtuous life. Now, trash the trash.

> God wants you to live a pure life. Keep yourselves from sexual promiscuity. Learn to appreciate and give dignity to your body, not abusing it, as is so common among those who know nothing of God.... God hasn't invited us into a disorderly, unkempt life but into something holy and beautiful—as beautiful on the inside as the outside. (1 Thessalonians 4:3–5, 7, *The Message*).

Write this Scripture in your journal or on an index card. If you're using index cards, put last week's card in your treasure box. Post this week's card where you'll see it. Here are a few other verses to ponder as well: Psalm 119:9; Matthew 5:8; 2 Corinthians 11:2; Philippians 4:8; and 1 Timothy 4:12.

Pretty Is As Pretty Does

*She had to complete twelve months of beauty treatments
prescribed for the women, six months with oil of myrrh
and six with perfumes and cosmetics.*

ESTHER 2:12

**READ CHAPTER 3 IN "FOR SUCH A TIME AS THIS."
READ ESTHER 2:12–14.**

A day or two at a spa sounds pretty great, but a whole year seems a bit extreme—especially since Esther was already "lovely in form and features" (Esther 2:7). So why was this time so important?

Just like purity is about more than just virginity, beauty is about more than what is seen on the outside. Like purity, beauty has to do with character. And Esther's character is what we want to learn about and pursue.

For many people—especially women—*beauty* is a loaded word and stirs up all kinds of emotions. Does the idea of beauty make you feel frustrated, happy, content, insignificant, like you've got it made, or something else? Why do you think that is?

Have you ever been judged because of how you looked or dressed? How did that make you feel?

THE BEAUTY BALANCING ACT

If you've grown up in the church or around Christians, it's easy to get confused about beauty. On the one hand, God created beauty—so it's good. On the other hand, we're told not to worry about how we look—so it's bad. Remember what Peter said?

> What matters is not your outer appearance—the styling of your hair, the jewelry you wear, the cut of your clothes—but your inner disposition. Cultivate inner beauty, the gentle, gracious kind that God delights in. The holy women of old were beautiful before God that way. (1 Peter 3:3–5, *The Message*)

How have you balanced verses like these with a desire to be attractive or pretty?

On a scale of one to five, are you so afraid that caring for your appearance is sinful that you just don't care how you look, or are you overly conscious of your appearance? (1 = not giving enough attention to appearance; 5 = giving too much attention to appearance.)

1   2   3   4   5

A BITTERSWEET SENSATION

Esther's year-long makeover did more than clear up her skin and whiten her teeth. It was also a process of purification and preparation for what was coming next. The bitter myrrh used to purify Esther's skin symbolizes the way the Holy Spirit purifies us for God. Sweet perfumes and cosmetics polished and refined Esther's beauty. Our prayers and worship are incense—sweet perfume—to God. Our character is refined as we spend time with Him.

God's kind of beauty requires both bitter and sweet.

Think about some of the difficult experiences that have shaped your character. It could be learning a hard lesson, going through tragedy, being humbled, or something else. Describe the situation using the idea of the bitter and the sweet. How did each of those elements affect your character?

Do you think looking at hard times this way—as an opportunity to build beautiful character—will change how you approach difficult situations in the future? Why or why not?

RISE UP

As you go through the upcoming week, think about balancing beauty. Write in your journal some ways you can enhance inner *and* outer beauty and how you can look beyond appearance to the beauty inside the people around you. Is there someone you have judged because of how she looks?

"Looks aren't everything. Don't be impressed with…looks and stature…. GOD judges persons differently than humans do. Men and women look at the face; GOD looks into the heart." (1 Samuel 16:7, *The Message*)

"As water reflects a face, so a man's [woman's] heart reflects the man [woman]." (Proverbs 27:19)

Add these verses to your journal. These are also great ones to put on your mirror—and keep there!

Set Apart...with Friends

The girl pleased him [Hegai] and won his favor.
Immediately he provided her... beauty treatments and special food.
He assigned to her seven maids selected from the king's palace and
moved her and her maids into the best place in the harem.

ESTHER 2:9

READ CHAPTERS 4–5 IN "FOR SUCH A TIME AS THIS."
READ ESTHER 2:8–9.

Esther knew she was different from the other women in the palace. After all, she was a Jew among pagans. She probably felt different and wondered why in the world she was there. Then to top it all off, Hegai—the pageant coordinator—singled her out for preferential treatment and moved her away from everyone else.

How do you think Esther felt about all of the changes going on in her life? How do you suppose the other women reacted to Esther's position as Hegai's favorite?

THE BEST PLACE

Being set apart is part of what being a Christian is all about. In His eyes, being set apart is necessary to becoming more like Christ.

Look up the words *set* and *apart*. Share your definitions with the group. Based on those two definitions, write a group definition for *being set apart*.

In what ways are you set apart?

How do you feel about being set apart? Does it make you feel special, trapped, or somewhere in between? Why?

Look up the words *sanctify* and *consecrate* in the dictionary, and read 1 Corinthians 6:11 in the Bible. What are some ways you might need to be more set apart for God in your life? Do you need to be set apart in your behavior? The way you talk? Your time? The way you dress? Something else? How can your friends help you take action?

SET APART, BUT NOT ALONE

Women are relational creatures. We travel in packs, love to talk, and need each other's advice. Esther was no different. And although Hegai may have set Esther up to be envied and even disliked by the other girls, he was a pretty smart guy in other ways. He knew she needed companions she could count on.

Look up and write the definition of the word *friend*.

What is your definition of a perfect friendship?

Think about a time when you faced crisis, felt set apart, or needed courage to "do the right thing" in an Esther moment. What difference did a friend make at that time?

Look at this:

He who walks with the wise grows wise, but a companion of fools suffers harm. (Proverbs 13:20)

What are some ways you can help your friends become wise? How does this group contribute to your quest for wisdom?

BAD COMPANY

We've all had them—friends who influence us the wrong way. And when it comes to being set apart, these friends don't help at all.

> You were running superbly! Who cut in on you, deflecting you from the true course of obedience? This detour doesn't come from the One who called you into the race in the first place. And please don't toss this off as insignificant. It only takes a minute amount of yeast, you know, to permeate an entire loaf of bread. (Galatians 5:7–9, *The Message*)

How does bad company influence you?

Think about a "minefield" or a "mission field" friend. How can this group help you either back away from her or stay strong as you reach out to her?

Look up the "friendship formula" on pages 68–69 of *For Such a Time as This*. Share what you appreciate about the "maiden" friends you have—especially those in this group. How can you be a better maiden friend?

RISE UP

Ask God to help you work specifically on one area of being set apart in your life this week. Record your thoughts in a journal throughout the week and then share with the group your results when you get together again. In what other ways can you—as an individual and as a group—be set apart?

Know that the LORD has set apart the godly for himself; the LORD will hear when I call to him. (Psalm 4:3)

"Before I formed you in the womb I knew you, before you were born I set you apart." (Jeremiah 1:5)

Write these verses in your journal or on an index card to be added to your card file. To remind you that you have been set apart for God for a holy and sanctified purpose just like the instruments of worship in the Old Testament temple were, attach a picture of yourself to another index card on which you have written these Scriptures and place it in your room. You might even want to frame this one to remind you of how special you are to God.

The Blessings of Obedience

For Esther obeyed the command of Mordecai as
when she was brought up by him.

ESTHER 2:20, NKJV

READ CHAPTER 6 IN "FOR SUCH A TIME AS THIS."
READ ESTHER 2:5–7, 10–11, 20.

One of the things we learn from Esther's story is that everyone has to obey someone. And because Esther learned to obey early on, obedience wasn't a lesson she had to learn the hard way later. From Esther 2:20, we see that obeying Mordecai about keeping her nationality a secret wasn't a one-time event. It was a pattern.

Look up and write down the definition of the word *obedient*.

What are some of man's laws you must obey?

Whose leadership do you have to honor, submit to, and obey?

Obedience Versus Lip Service

Obedience isn't just about our actions. It's also about *attitude*. And although the act of obedience is important, God places a high value on how we obey—something most of us struggle with at one time or another.

Think of a time when you obeyed but didn't want to. Describe the feelings/emotions you felt about the situation.

In order to honor and obey an authority figure, what aspect of negative character do you have to let go of? Pride? Control? Selfishness?

What beautiful character do you have to call on? Trust? Self-Control? Patience?

What are some of the blessings of obedience that are described in the following Scriptures: Exodus 19:5–6 and 20:12; Leviticus 25:18; Proverbs 19:16; John 15:10; Ephesians 6:1–3; 1 John 3:24?

Take another look at this paragraph from *For Such a Time as This*:

> You cannot obey and submit to your heavenly Father if you have not learned to listen to and obey earthly authority. Your ability to be obedient in horizontal relationships with man is directly related to your ability to be obedient in a vertical relationship with God.[1]

How can you use heartfelt obedience to those in authority over you—your parents, your boss, a teacher—as a way to get ready to obey God?

Based on the way you obey the people in your life, how ready are you to obey God when He asks you to do something hard? Scary? Bigger than you?

A PERFECT EXAMPLE OF OBEDIENCE

Esther did a pretty good job with obedience—perhaps she had a good example to follow like Mordecai's wife, a teacher, or a friend. We also have an example to follow—one of perfect obedience.

While He lived on earth, how did Jesus demonstrate obedience and respect to His heavenly Father? Find some specific examples.

Jesus was obedient even unto death, resulting in favor, promotion, and position (see Philippians 2:8–11). How are you blessed by His obedience?

RISE UP

Ask God to give you an attitude of obedience this week. In your journal, record how your attitude toward obeying authority figures changed throughout the week, for better or worse.

"Do you think all GOD wants are sacrifices—empty rituals just for show? He wants you to listen to him! Plain listening is the thing, not staging a lavish religious production." (1 Samuel 15:22, *The Message*)

Don't forget to add this Scripture to your collection.

Get Real!

Each young woman went to the king, and she was given whatever
she desired to take with her from the women's quarters....
She [Esther] requested nothing but what Hegai...advised.

ESTHER 2:13, 15, NKJV

READ CHAPTER 7 IN "FOR SUCH A TIME AS THIS."
READ ESTHER 2:13–16.

The time approached for all the young women to be presented to King Xerxes. Can you picture the scene? Everyone running around...trying on different clothes, hairstyles, and even personalities. Each woman was determined to be exactly what the king wanted—even if it wasn't who she really was. All except Esther.

What do you think it would have been like to be part of this scene? Would you have enjoyed it? Why or why not?

Now imagine you're Esther. What's running through your mind?

JUST BE YOURSELF

"Just be yourself" seems like pretty simple advice. But it can be hard to follow, especially since we have so many options for hiding who we really are.

What does it mean to be "real?" Look up the word *real* in the dictionary, and then share your own definition with the group.

Think of a situation where you had a hard time being yourself—the first day of school, a first date, or a particular occasion with friends. Why was it so hard to be yourself?

When you find yourself in those situations, what's the mask you hide behind? Remember that hiding doesn't always mean being less noticeable (like being shy); sometimes hiding behind something makes people pay more attention (like being funny).

What are some ways you could lay that mask aside? Since getting rid of a mask can be scary or hard, think about and record here some practical steps you can take to be *real*.

BEING CONTENT WITH THE REAL YOU

No matter how we try to hide, God knows who we really are. Although we know that He loves us, it can be hard to be happy with the way that He made us. Instead of grounding our identity in Him, we find our identity in other things.

What things do you find your identity in?

Look at "Get Real with Your Bad Self" on page 86 of *For Such a Time as This*. Write a list of the aspects of the "real you" that you hide from others.

RISE UP

God wants us to be real with Him. He already knows everything about us—and loves us anyway! More than anything, He longs for our hearts to be open and vulnerable to Him so He can transform us into His image.

As you go through this week, pick one way you want to be more real with the people around you. Was it harder or easier than you thought it would be? Why?

We don't yet see things clearly. We're squinting in a fog, peering through a mist. But it won't be long before the weather clears and the sun shines bright! We'll see it all then, see it all as clearly as God sees us, knowing him directly just as he knows us! (1 Corinthians 13:12, *The Message*)

In your journal or on the back of your Scripture card for this week, write a prayer asking God to help you be real with Him and others. Share with Him any specific areas you struggle with and ask for His healing. As you meditate on and memorize this Scripture this week, ask God to help you more clearly understand His love for you.

Finding Favor for Position

Esther found favor in the eyes of all who saw her....
The king loved Esther more than all the women, and she found favor and
kindness with him more than all the virgins, so that he set the royal crown
on her head and made her queen instead of Vashti.

ESTHER 2:15, 17, NASB

READ CHAPTERS 8–9 IN "FOR SUCH A TIME AS THIS."
READ ESTHER 2:17–18.

It can be easy to confuse favor with popularity—having lots of friends and being envied by everyone around us. Looking at Esther's story can help us understand what favor really is and what kind of favor is most important. Although Esther did win the favor of everyone around her, the important idea here is that she had *God's* favor. And that's the favor that counts.

Look up the word *favor* in the dictionary.

After reading chapter 8 in *For Such a Time as This*, how would you define *favor?*

chooses to give rather than receive. Hospitality invests in relationships.... The power of hospitality is in serving others."[6] How did Esther do each of these things through her dinner party?

To commemorate the coming completion of this study, firm up your plans for having an "Esther banquet." (Lots of young women have told me about how they have personalized their banquets with official invitations, formal dresses, promise ring ceremonies, limousines, food preparation, and fund-raisers.) Get creative and personalize your own Esther banquet! Present yourselves as princesses in God's court.

RISE UP

How can you show hospitality to one person this week? Think about a specific person. Perhaps someone who is not typically included or even a person you don't like (you know, that whole "love your enemies" idea). As you ask God to guide you, keep in mind how Esther displayed discernment. Be ready next week to share with the group how it went.

Then Jesus said to his host, "When you give a luncheon or dinner, do not invite your friends, your brothers or relatives, or your rich neighbors.... But when you give a banquet, invite the poor, the crippled, the lame, the blind, and you will be blessed." (Luke 14:12–14)

As you memorize and meditate on these verses this week, ask God to show you some creative ways to express the heart of hospitality and service to others.

As seen in the lives of Esther, Joseph (see Genesis 39), Daniel (see Daniel 1–2), and Mary (see Luke 1), obedience always precedes favor. Also, read and reflect again on the example of Christ's life (see Philippians 2:8–11) that we focused on in week 5, "The Blessings of Obedience." Read through their stories together and look for the pattern of "obedience-favor-promotion-position-purpose" in their lives.

How would you describe the link between obedience and favor? How did God favor these people? In what ways did His favor benefit more than just one individual? Share with the group what you learn.

Have you seen this pattern of "obedience-favor-promotion-positon-purpose" at work in your own life? If so, how?

GOD'S FAVOR

As we can see in these sentences taken from *For Such a Time as This,* God's favor on Esther didn't just benefit her; it was for the good of an entire nation. "If God's favor is resting on you, it's not about you…. God does not grant His favor just for the good of one person. It's always because He wants to use that one person to advance His Kingdom."[2]

Make a list of the ways God has favored you—it could be in your relationships, your intelligence, your talent, your personality, or other ways.
How does God's favor in those areas of your life advance His Kingdom?
How can you use that favor to share your faith or encourage other
believers?

POSITIONED FOR A PURPOSE

"Divine favor always leads to greater position and responsibility as we walk
out our destiny."[3] God's favor led Esther to a palace and a crown, but it also
led her to a crisis and a call to be an advocate for God's people. She is still
celebrated today, in the Jewish Feast of Purim, for saving a nation. Imagine
where God's favor could lead you!

Make a list of the positions you hold—at home, school, church, work,
and so on.

Think about this: How you respond to each of your positions determines when you're ready to move on to greater position or more responsibility. How are you responding to each of the positions you're in?

RISE UP

Because you are a "princess in God's court," you already have God's favor. Are you living up to your position as His daughter? Are you ready to ask Him for more? As you meditate on these questions throughout the week, ask God to show you at least one new way you could respond *responsibly* this week to each of the positions you're in.

I urge you to live a life worthy of the calling you have received. (Ephesians 4:1)

In your journal or on the back of your Scripture card for this week, list the people who you think will be positively affected by your choices to walk worthy of your calling.

Crisis!

"Do not think in your heart that you will escape in the king's palace
any more than all the other Jews. For if you remain completely silent at this time,
relief and deliverance will arise for the Jews from another place,
but you and your father's house will perish."

ESTHER 4:13–14, NKJV

READ CHAPTERS 10–11 IN "FOR SUCH A TIME AS THIS."
READ ESTHER 3:1—4:14.

L ife seems to be going pretty well for Esther. She's the queen, her cousin Mordecai is still close by, and she's won the favor of everyone around her. But you know how it goes. Just when you think things are going great— *pow!*—out of the blue, a new challenge emerges.

Describe a time when suddenly you were faced with a crisis in your life. How did you respond?

CRISIS OR OPPORTUNITY?

"Every cloud has a silver lining" sounds pretty trite when faced with a storm cloud. But sayings like this one exist because they're true (as much as we hate to hear it!). The fact is this: Each crisis we face is an opportunity to build character and show the world (and ourselves) exactly what we're made of.

> Whenever trouble comes your way, let it be an opportunity for joy. For when your faith is tested, your endurance has a chance to grow. So let it grow, for when your endurance is fully developed, you will be strong in character and ready for anything. (James 1:2–4, NLT)

What is produced in us when we face crisis with faith?

> But we have this treasure in jars of clay to show that this all-surpassing power is from God and not from us. We are hard pressed on every side, but not crushed; perplexed, but not in despair; persecuted, but not abandoned; struck down, but not destroyed. (2 Corinthians 4:7–9)

Think of this treasure as your character—the character of Christ that God is forming in you. What do you learn about that treasure from these verses?

Think about this: No one can see what's inside a clay jar unless it's cracked. Think about the crisis you described. How did the cracks from that crisis allow others to see your character, good or bad?

GOD THE DIRECTOR

Most of us can relate to Esther on this. She faced a big, huge, enormous decision and waited for God's voice to come booming down from the clouds, telling her exactly what she should do. And she waited. And she waited. Ever felt like that before?

Read "Picture This" on pages 124–126 in *For Such a Time as This*. Now think about the story of your life. Spend some time thinking about how God has directed your life so far. Now, write in your journal your own quick script like this one.

Go back to the crisis you described at the beginning of this week's study. How do you think God prepared you—spiritually, physically, emotionally—for that time in your life? Be specific.

Two Views of Life

You have a choice. You can look at a crisis—or any event in your life—as coincidence, chance, and random, *or* you can see it as part of God's plan and direction for your life.

Talk with the group about some challenging things you're facing or have faced. Contrast the two ways of viewing those situations. How can you choose to look at the circumstances you are facing?

Rise Up

We can be sure that hard times will come (see John 16:33). But we can also be sure that we don't have to face them alone. Spend some time meditating on the verse below. How has God protected, sustained, and strengthened you in the past as you've faced a crisis? How will He protect you in the future?

So do not fear, for I am with you; do not be dismayed, for I am your God. I will strengthen you and help you; I will uphold you with my righteous right hand. (Isaiah 41:10)

Write this Scripture in your journal or on an index card. Also, write one way you will courageously face up to a difficulty that you have been avoiding in the past. When you achieve your recorded goal, insert that card in your treasure box or make a note of it in your journal.

Divine Destiny

*"For if you remain silent at this time, relief and deliverance for the Jews
will arise from another place, but you and your father's family will perish.
And who knows but that you have come to royal position for such a time as this?"*

ESTHER 4:14

**READ CHAPTER 12 IN "FOR SUCH A TIME AS THIS."
READ ESTHER 4:1–14.**

Destiny. With Mordecai's emphatic words, Esther knew it was time to face hers. Haman's scheming had gone far enough, and the lives of every Jew that Esther knew—and every Jew she didn't—were on the line. It was up to her to act.

God's direction brought her to a pivotal point in her life. Esther could face her destiny and approach the king to save her people, or she could sit back and stay silent.

Look up definitions for *destiny* and *destination*.

How do you think Esther would have defined her choice at this point in time (see Esther 4:13–14)?

WHAT'S YOUR PURPOSE?

Sometimes the word *destiny* can be overwhelming. So try this on: "Personal destiny does not lie in any one position, place, or event. It's in the purpose."[4] Destiny is about answering the question why.

What's your purpose? Think beyond the positions you hold, the places you find yourself, and the events you attend. What's the desire that remains constant wherever you are and whoever you're with?

Try this as you're thinking about your destiny. What are some of the gifts and talents God has given you? How does using them fit into what you think about your destiny?

LITTLE MOMENTS OF DESTINY

For many of us, facing destiny doesn't come down to one life-altering decision. Instead, destiny is about adding up the small and seemingly inconsequential choices we make as we go through each day.

"You can tell a lot about where you are going by looking at where you've been."[5] Look back at Esther's story. How did events in her life lead her to this point of facing her destiny?

What are some decisions or events that define your destiny? (These decisions could be how you spend your time, whom you choose for friends, how you've handled crisis, what goals you've set, and so on.) How are these decisions actually destiny points along your path?

How can having purpose affect how you go through your typical day? Be as specific as possible.

A DATE WITH DESTINY

Part of the destiny we all share is to become more and more like Jesus. That's God's greatest purpose for us, His daughters. At the same time, God uses our unique destinies to accomplish great things for His kingdom.

> And we know that in all things God works for the good of those who love him, who have been called according to his purpose. For those God foreknew he also predestined to be conformed to the likeness of his Son. (Romans 8:28–29)

What are some of the ways God is conforming you "to the likeness of his Son"?

How does this group help fulfill God's purpose for you? Are there additional things the group could do to help you discover and live out your purpose? How can you help someone else discover and live out her purpose?

RISE UP

Think back to week 7 and the positions you hold. How has your life up to this point prepared you "for such a time as this" in the positions you hold now?

> And who knows but that you have come to [this] position for such a time as this? (Esther 4:14)

As you write down the Scripture to meditate on this week, also write down the critical, destiny-shaping moments in your life that seem to be approaching and how you will face them.

Choices Matter

READ CHAPTER 13 IN "FOR SUCH A TIME AS THIS."
READ ESTHER 4:12–15.

Throughout Esther's story, there are lots of opportunities for us to wish the author had included a little more information. And this is definitely one of those times. What happened between verses 14 and 15? What did Esther do, think, feel, and pray? How did she make her choice?

If you were Esther, how would you have spent the time between those verses? How do you make tough decisions?

DECIDING AND DOING

There's no foolproof, perfect process for making a hard decision. But making smaller decisions each day gives us practice before it's time to make a really, really big one.

Flip back through Esther's story. What specific choices has she made up to this point? How does each of those decisions prepare her for this one big one?

Now look back on your life so far. What are some of the decisions you've made? How do you think those decisions influenced the course of your life? How do they relate to your purpose or destiny?

LITTLE CHOICES, LIFE CHOICES

The way we approach daily choices can have a big effect on the way we approach larger life choices.

List at least ten choices you made today—big and small. Which ones were more difficult for you to make? Why?

What big life choices are *you* facing now? How has making good "every-day" decisions in the past affected your ability to make a good decision now?

Good Choices, Bad Choices

Although we try to make good choices, nobody's perfect. There are times when we'll make horrible decisions and wonder how to get back on track. Luckily, God is a redeemer and uses even our bad choices to prepare us to meet our destinies.

What are some of the poor choices you've made? Do they have anything in common (other than just being bad!)?

What did you learn from making those choices?

How has God redeemed those choices in your life?

Although a particular choice of ours may not seem as big as Esther's, we all have choices to make that affect our destinies. God won't force us to make good choices. Nonetheless, the choices we make do matter—big or small. At the end of each day this week, record in your journal one additional way you have chosen to serve God and pursue His destiny/purpose in your life.

> "But if serving the LORD seems undesirable to you, then choose for yourselves this day whom you will serve…. But as for me and my household, we will serve the LORD." (Joshua 24:15)

Choosing to ask Jesus to be the Lord and Savior of your life is the biggest and most important choice you can make. Would you like to make that choice? Or do you need to choose to rededicate your life wholeheartedly? If so, this is your date with destiny. As you write this Scripture out, take a minute to talk to God about where you are with Him. Write down your thoughts.

Stand in the Gap

*[Mordecai] told [Esther's servant] to urge her to go into the king's presence
to beg for mercy and plead with him for her people.... Then Esther
sent this reply to Mordecai: "Go, gather together all the Jews who are in Susa,
and fast for me. Do not eat or drink for three days, night or day.
I and my maids will fast as you do. When this is done,
I will go to the king.... And if I perish, I perish."*

ESTHER 4:8, 15–16

**READ CHAPTERS 14–15 IN "FOR SUCH A TIME AS THIS."
READ ESTHER 4:1–17.**

Esther made her choice. She would seize her destiny and stand in the gap to intercede with the king on behalf of her people. She would be an advocate against the injustice that was about to happen—the total annihilation of every Jew in the country.

What can we learn from Esther about what it means to stand in the gap—to be an advocate—for others?

What price was Esther willing to pay to embrace her destiny and do the right thing—the God thing?

Can you think of some other people throughout history who have stood in the gap for others—people who have taken up a cause for the sake of others?

What are some characteristics that these people share with each other and with Esther?

ADVOCACY 101

So what does it look like to be an advocate? Chances are we may never have to approach the Supreme Court to fight for the lives of our families and friends. At the same time, being an advocate is something we can do most every day.

Grab a dictionary. What does the word *advocate* mean?

Describe a time when you stood up against injustice. It could be something big or small. How did standing in the gap make you feel? Did the situation require personal sacrifice as Esther's did? Was there a potential price to pay?

Now think of a time when you stood back and did nothing. Was there a cost to your inaction? How did that make you feel? Do you wish you'd reacted differently? If so, how?

An Advocate like Jesus

Take a look at this:

> So, what do you think? With God on our side like this, how can we lose? If God didn't hesitate to put everything on the line for us, embracing our condition and exposing himself to the worst by sending his own Son, is there anything else he wouldn't gladly and freely do for us? And who would dare tangle with God by messing with one of God's chosen? Who would dare even to point a finger? The One who died for us—who was raised to life for us!—is in the presence of God at this very moment sticking up for us. Do you think anyone is going to be able to drive a wedge between us and Christ's love for us? There is no way! Not trouble, not hard times, not hatred, not hunger, not homelessness, not bullying threats, not backstabbing. (Romans 8:31–35, *The Message*)

What do you learn from Jesus about being an advocate?

DOING YOUR HOMEWORK

Before you face a challenging situation, it's always a good idea to get prepared. That's exactly what Esther did. She faced her choice, evaluated the cost, made her decision to stand in the gap, and got ready to act. How? She fasted and she prayed—two things that focused her mind entirely on God.

After reading chapter 15 in *For Such a Time as This,* how would you describe the link between fasting and prayer?

RISE UP

Try a three-day fast this week. Pick something to give up and something to pray for in its place. It could be a situation you're facing, an injustice you want to be an advocate for, or a relationship you're struggling with. Be prepared to share with the group how fasting and prayer changed your perspective and the situation.

So we fasted and petitioned our God about this, and he answered our prayer. (Ezra 8:23)

Be sure to copy this Scripture into your journal or on an index card. Also, write insights the Lord gives you as you meditate on this Scripture and fast and pray this week.

For an added reminder, write the verse on an extra card. Then, if you're fasting from a food item, put the card on the refrigerator or pantry. If you are fasting from television, magazines, the phone, or something else, put the card where it will remind you to pray in a moment of temptation.

Now Serving

Esther answered, "If it pleases the king, let the king and Haman come today to the banquet that I have prepared for him."

ESTHER 5:4, NKJV

READ CHAPTER 16 IN "FOR SUCH A TIME AS THIS."
READ ESTHER 5:1-8; 7:1-10.

After praying and fasting for three days, why did Esther throw a dinner party and invite the enemy? It just goes to show you what happens when you ask the God of creativity for a solution to your crisis. His ways are not our ways.

The key idea here is serving through hospitality. It was part of Esther's character. Look up *hospitality* in the dictionary. Based on what you've learned about Esther so far, what would you add to the definition?

HOSPITALITY 101

The key to practicing hospitality isn't a lifelong subscription to *Martha Stewart Living*. Here it is: "Hospitality puts others before itself. Hospitality

Courage for Generation Esther

"Rise up; this matter is in your hands.
We will support you, so take courage and do it."

EZRA 10:4

READ CHAPTER 17 AND THE EPILOGUE IN "FOR
SUCH A TIME AS THIS."
READ ESTHER (JUST ONE MORE TIME!).

One of Esther's greatest tests of character was courage. What did Esther need courage to do? What was she afraid of? What was the outcome of Esther's courage and boldness?

COURAGE 101

Okay, it's math time. Look at this equation and explain it in your own words:

$$Courage = Faith > Fear$$

PUTTING IT ALL TOGETHER

We need courage to develop character. Nothing we've talked about so far comes easily. It takes courage to be pure, to be set apart, to obey, to get real, to face crisis and destiny, to make good choices, to be an advocate for others, to put ourselves on the line, and to reach out and serve others.

Look back through each week of this study. Where do you need courage in the development of your character?

How can you take courage in one area of your life this week? What aspect of the situation do you fear?

Remember, "Courage is not a feeling. Courage is a choice."[7]

So be strong and take courage, all you who put your hope in the Lord! (Psalm 31:24, NLT)

Write this Scripture and the previous quote on one of your index cards or in your journal. Also write the step of courage you plan to take this week and the thing in the situation you fear. After you have acted courageously in this situation, write the date and the outcome of the situation. How did this act of courage make you feel?

GENERATION ESTHER

Together we've made it through the book of Esther and *For Such a Time as This*. We've learned some things about what it takes to live virtuously, practice faith courageously, and be set apart completely. It's important to review what we've learned so we can continue to put it into practice.

Go back and read through your answers in this study guide. What's one new thing you've learned from doing this study? How has that changed you?

YOU ARE NOT ALONE

Are you ready to join the ranks of women who are part of Generation Esther?

Reflect on your experience as a group. How did this group make doing the study better than doing it alone?

What are some ways you can stay accountable to each other about the things you've learned from Esther?

Take some time to talk about the "Esther" you see in each other. How does each person in the group reflect an aspect of Esther's character? What have you learned from each other about character, courage, purpose, and destiny?

Finally, talk about the future of your group. Do you want to have an Esther banquet? Do you want to continue and study another book together? Do you want to start a new study of Esther with some different people? Do you want to become a leader yourself?

RISE UP

Reflect on this last verse together. As a group, come up with a definition of what it means to be a modern-day Esther and write it down as you have throughout this study. Agree to help each other take courage and be living definitions of a modern-day Esther.

Rise up; this matter is in your hands. We will support you, so
take courage and do it. (Ezra 10:4)

Finally, in your journal, record the steps that God has taken you through as you have been emerging as a modern-day Esther. Then rise up and take the words you have written over the course of this study and live them out as you fulfill your part in Generation Esther.

Notes

1. Lisa Ryan, *For Such a Time as This* (Sisters, Ore.: Multnomah Publishers, 2001), 77.

2. Ibid., 94.

3. Ibid., 96.

4. Ibid., 137.

5. Ibid., 138.

6. Ibid., 177.

7. Ibid., 189.